KID SCIENTIST
Marine Biologists on a Dive

Sue Fliess

illustrated by Mia Powell

Albert Whitman & Company
Chicago, Illinois

To Mom and Dad, for encouraging me to be
anything I wanted to be—SF

For my wonderful friends and family—MP

Library of Congress Cataloging-in-Publication data
is on file with the publisher.

Text copyright © 2022 by Sue Fliess
Illustrations copyright © 2022 by Albert Whitman & Company
Illustrations by Mia Powell
First published in the United States of America
in 2022 by Albert Whitman & Company
ISBN 978-0-8075-4158-6 (hardcover)
ISBN 978-0-8075-4156-2 (ebook)

Printed in China
10 9 8 7 6 5 4 3 2 1 WKT 26 25 24 23 22 21

For more information about Albert Whitman & Company,
visit our website at www.albertwhitman.com.

"Ready?" Maggie asks.

Her small team of marine biologists gives a thumbs up. Maggie pops in her mouthpiece, checks her scuba gear, and flips backward off the research boat into the water.

Splash!

They dive down.

Marine biologists are scientists that study plant and animal life in the ocean. After months of researching humpback whales, this team is finally starting their field study by swimming with whales!

Maggie and her team have timed their trip during the humpback pod's, or group's, migration—the seasonal movement from one area to another. This lets the team study these amazing creatures in their natural surroundings.

In the water, each scientist has a different job based on what they want to research.

Jacob takes notes and sketches in his underwater notebook, which has waterproof pages.

Lucia collects plankton samples with a plankton net. Plankton are tiny living marine organisms carried along by tides and currents. Lucia hopes to catch and examine krill, the type of plankton humpbacks eat. The health of the krill will help her learn about the health of the ocean habitat.

Arjun films the whales so he can study their behavior later. Jasmine photographs them.

But Maggie hopes to record a whale song.

Maggie knows that all whales click, whistle, and slap their tails on the water to communicate. But whale songs are different, and only the males sing. A song can sound like a moan, a door closing, a bark, or even a cry—and these sounds have a melody.

Maggie wants to know how their songs are formed.

She has a hypothesis, or a prediction based on evidence, that the whales sing by stringing together combinations of these musical sounds in a repeated pattern. If Maggie can record whale songs today, she'll be able to listen to and analyze them back in the lab.

Maggie and the team keep a safe distance from the pod.
Maggie turns on her underwater microphone, called a hydrophone.
She listens and waits.

CLICK
CLICK - C

OAAAAeeClick

The team collects the data they need, but as they begin to board the boat again, Maggie hears a humpback slap her flukes, or tail fins, on the water's surface, which could be a sign of a threat. Maggie swims back down for another look.

A fishing net is tangled around a young whale's fin!

She and Jacob swim toward the trapped whale. The two carefully cut through the fishing net, freeing the fin. The calf swims back to its mother, which hovers in front of Maggie, as if to say thank you, before swimming off. The scientists head back to the boat with the netting.

"That was unbelievable!" says Lucia.

Arjun replies, "I'm so glad we were here to help. And now we really have a *tale* to tell."

The team cheers.

Jacob inspects the netting. "I wonder if this is from local fishermen."

"Since this pod is migrating," says Maggie, "the whale could have been caught in the net somewhere else along the journey."

The team agrees to investigate in town later.

Back in the lab, the team analyzes the data they've gathered. Jacob transfers his notes to the computer. "I noticed one female was acting strangely," he says.

"Maybe that was the tangled calf's mother," replies Maggie.

Lucia studies her plankton sample under the microscope.

"The plankton looks healthy," she says.

Arjun takes a look. "Nutritious *and* delicious!" he laughs.

Jasmine sifts through the photos she's taken. "Look at all the scars on the mother and calf," she says.

"Sometimes," says Jacob, "orca whales attack young humpbacks while they are migrating. It can leave them pretty scratched up."

They all gather to watch Arjun's video footage, observing
the whales filling up on food and continuing to migrate north.
"I hope this pod makes the journey safely," says Lucia.

Maggie's hydrophone recorded the sound waves from the whale song. Sound travels in waves, which carry sound to the ear. Maggie listens for a repeating pattern.

Soon she detects three recognizable noises: a low moan, followed by a sound like a creaking door, and finally, a high-pitched squeal. The three sounds are repeating in a pattern!

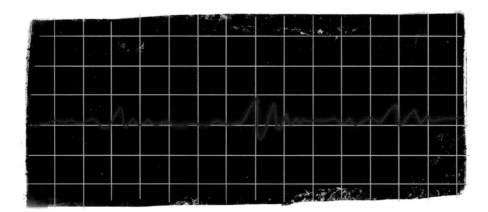

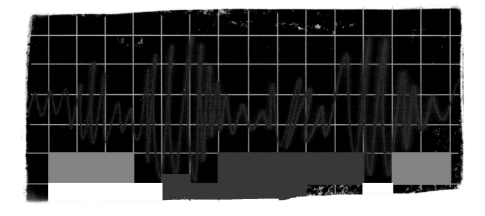

Maggie is excited, and this is good evidence to support her hypothesis that whale songs are made up of repeating sound patterns, but she will have to record more whale songs to confirm it.

The team wraps up their study in the area and prepares to present their findings to other marine biologists at an upcoming conference. They hope the data they gathered will teach others more about humpback whales.

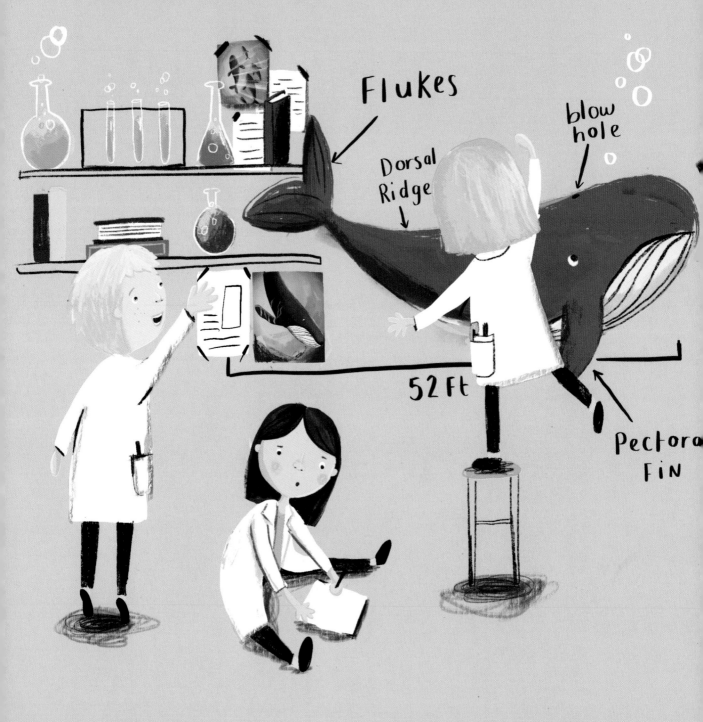

Maggie will never forget how it felt to study these awesome creatures and help a young calf swim free.

"Hmm," Maggie wonders.
"What should we dive into next?"

WHAT IS A MARINE BIOLOGIST?

Marine biology is the scientific study of plants, animals, and other living things found in the ocean. Marine biologists study the behavior, lives, diseases, and habitats of all marine animals and organisms. There are more than 200,000 different marine species, which include fungi and bacteria.

Marine biologists do lots of research on land *before* they get to do hands-on field research in the water. This includes reading and studying marine science, applying for grants, or money to pay for research, and learning how to approach live animals. After they've completed a study, marine biologists publish papers about what they have found in their research. Sometimes marine biologists also bring students into the field for hands-on learning.

All scientists research by following the steps of the scientific method. Maggie and her team used each step to guide their research.

STEPS OF THE SCIENTIFIC METHOD

1. Make an observation and do background research. Before Maggie and her team went swimming with whales, they did research on humpback whales from afar.

2. Ask questions about the observations and gather information. After hearing whale songs, Maggie asked how and why whales sing.

3. Form a hypothesis. Maggie hypothesized that whale songs are made from repeating patterns of sound.

4. Perform an experiment and collect data. Maggie and her team swam with whales to collect recordings of a whale song.

5. Analyze the data and draw conclusions. Consider how the conclusions support or disprove the hypothesis. Maggie's analysis showed that the whale song she recorded was made up of repeating sounds. This supported her hypothesis.

6. Communicate or present your findings. After gathering more data, Maggie and her team will publish their research so others can learn more about humpback whales and the sounds they make.

HOW CAN I BECOME A MARINE BIOLOGIST?

Do you love the ocean and all its creatures? Maybe you'll be a marine biologist!

There are so many ways to learn about marine biology, even before you study it in school:

- Check out books at your local library or visit a nearby aquarium or zoo.
- Take a whale-watching excursion with your family.
- Find out if you have a marine wildlife rescue center near you where you can talk to a guide and possibly see some marine life, such as otters, seals, or sea turtles, being rehabilitated to return to their natural habitats.
- Go beachcombing or explore tidepools.

When you get older, if you decide you want to become a marine biologist, you can choose a college that lets you specialize in marine biology. You'll get both a classroom and hands-on field education. You can earn a bachelor of science (BS) degree in marine biology by completing four years of college. You'll study ocean geology, marine mammals, fish, plants, biological habitats, and the chemical makeup of water. You may learn about underwater photography, get a scuba certification, and even swim with whales, like Maggie!

SUGGESTED READING FOR KIDS

Gibson, Karen Bush, and Lena Chandhok. *Marine Biology: Cool Women Who Dive*. White River Junction, VT: Nomad, 2016.

Kelley, K. C. *Marine Biologists!* Broomall, PA: Mason Crest, 2016.

Koontz, Robin. *Marine Biologists*. Vero Beach, FL: Rourke, 2016.

Owen, Ruth. *Marine Biologists*. New York: PowerKids, 2014.